PROCESS THEOLOGY AND POLITICS

BRUCE G. EPPERLY

Topical Line Drives
Volume 43

Energion Publications
Gonzalez, Florida
2020

ISBN: 978-1-63199-624-5
eISBN: 978-1-63199-625-2

Energion Publications
PO Box 841
Gonzalez, FL 32560

https://energion.com
pubs@energion.com

TABLE OF CONTENTS

Chapter One

Healing Politics

"You don't ask questions when your house is on fire! You put it out!" a friend noted in the course of a conversation on the importance of theology in changing peoples' attitudes and behaviors toward climate change. I nodded in agreement as the conversation turned to the brush fires in Australia and the irony that a casualty of the unprecedented 2018 Northern California forest fires was the destruction of Paradise, a bucolic village that happened to be in the fire's path. Continuing his commentary, my friend lamented, "You remember the words of that Joni Mitchell song 'Pave paradise and put up a parking lot.' Now we're not only paving Paradise, we're choosing to incinerate our planet and rob our children and youth of their future. We need change and we need it now!"

As I pondered my friend's comments along with the widespread dismissal of Greta Thunberg and the Parkland School youth as unrealistic by USA political and religious leaders, I couldn't help but nod my head in agreement. "Yes, the planet is on fire, and we need to put it out! My grandchildren participate in active shooter drills at school. Women wearing hijabs are harassed at gas stations on Cape Cod where I live, and the USA has exited climate change and nuclear treaties, putting ideology and short-terms profits ahead of our children's future. Our nation is sick and we need healing." Little did I know that just a few months later the United States and virtually every other nation would be confronted by a global pandemic, challenging our assumptions about national sovereignty as well as American exceptionalism. And, in the middle of the pandemic, millions of Americans took to the streets, donning their masks, to protest the deaths of African Americans at the hands of law enforcement officials.

Looking at our current global and national situation, I must admit that my friend is right. When there's an emergency, you call 911 and do whatever you can to save your loved ones. Initially, there's no time for theological conversation in the middle of an emergency. Still, theology and spirituality are important in our personal lives and our response to the political and planetary crises we face. Our deepest beliefs shape how we view the world, the human prospect, and our ethical decision-making. Healthy and life-transforming theology changes minds and behaviors and leads us as persons and nations from death to life. Unhealthy theologies and racist ideologies, as we witnessed during the COVID-19 pandemic, promote destructive behaviors in relationship to the non-human world, people who differ from us, and our responsibility to our fellow citizens.

As we look at the political horizon in North America and across the globe, it is obvious that our civic lives need healing in terms of policy and practice. Our glorification of power and unrestrained consumption has put the earth in peril, widened the gap between rich and poor, and subverted the democratic structures of society. The alignment of authoritarian religion and politics has led to incivility, insult, and the binary denunciation of political opponents as unpatriotic and dangerous. Failure to appreciate the importance of pluralism and scientific research combined with absolutizing our finite perspectives and prejudices has rendered the quest for common good peripheral to political calculation. We have succumbed to the politics of exclusion and binary incivility, when our national and planetary survival needs wider and wider circles of inclusion. In our quest for healing, we need to ponder the question, "who is our 'us'?" Who belongs and who is foreign? Who is necessary and who do we in our political certainty deem expendable?

WHEN THEOLOGY IS A MATTER OF LIFE OR DEATH

Theology matters. Among many Christians today, the humble Galilean origins of Christianity have been eclipsed by coercive and monolithic visions of Constantinian Christendom. Consider the recent Evangelicals for Trump rally in Florida.[1] Adoring Christians gathered as an American president boldly proclaimed "We have God on our side," denounced progressives and liberals as enemies of Christianity, and promised to restore Christianity to its rightful leadership of American society through reinstituting prayer in

---

1   https://www.breitbart.com/politics/2020/01/03/donald-trump-rallies-evangelicals-in-florida-we-have-god-on-our-side/

public schools, maintaining gun rights, rolling back laws providing equal rights to the LGBTQ community, and promoting economic growth over environmental protection. Forgetting humankind's temptation toward idolatry, many conservative religious leaders proclaim that Donald Trump is God's "chosen one" and as he gazes heavenward, Trump seems to share their fantasy. In their minds, they embody God's chosen political agenda, promoted by God's chosen people, and with a clear mandate to shape the world according to their religious values. Consider the recent denunciation of scientific research and advice to practice physical distancing by megachurch pastors. Note also the damage caused by the widespread belief that the Coronavirus reflects divine punishment for America's growing acceptance of the LGBTQ community.

With Jesus' anticipated, but constantly recalibrated, second coming on the horizon, many of these same conservative evangelical and Pentecostal Christians, including some at the highest levels of USA government, believe that placing an American embassy in Jerusalem and saber-rattling in the Middle East will hasten the final battle between good and evil and bring about God's reign on earth. God and country, apocalypse and foreign policy, divine omnipotence, and climate denial have come together to create a perfect storm of conflict, polarization, and planetary destruction.

The absolutism, characteristic of apocalyptic and authoritarian theologies, whether in the United States or Iran, has fueled the flames of incivility in the halls of Congress, cable television, social media, and on city streets. Prizing their faith, scriptures, and authorities as absolute, many conservative Christians see any challenge to their beliefs and political agenda as coming from the influence of demonic forces. Alternative beliefs, lifestyles, and world views are dangerous to the "one, true faith and economic order" and those who question their norms are deemed infidels and unpatriotic, worthy not only of denunciation but, in some minds, eradication.

I write as a process theologian and pastor raised in the evangelical world to persons of faith who seek the healing of our nations and the planet. In my childhood, it was commonplace for revival preachers to begin their sermons with a message of bad news, and in the spirit of those Baptist preachers, I have portrayed a grim national and planetary picture, shaped in part by unhealthy theologies of absolutism that conflate authoritarian theological and political perspectives. Yet, in the revival tradition, after the bad news comes good news that we can be born again, change direction, and chart a new life for ourselves and the world.

Today, the path to national and planetary healing must be theological, ethical, and political. We do not have to conform to the world of authoritarian Christianity and its vision of a sovereign, punitive, and dominating God. We can be transformed by the Galilean vision of Christianity that treasures the earth, honors relationships, and prizes pluralism. We can discover God as the model for life-affirming relationships in a pluralistic and changing society. Encountering God as the engine of creativity, diversity, social justice, and earth care inspires us to prophetic healing in our political and cultural relationships.

I believe that process theology provides inspiration for shaping justice-oriented and earth-affirming political policies in a pluralistic culture. Following the Hebraic prophets, whose message was aimed at political and economic leaders, process theology affirms the need for social transformation. God invites us to let justice roll down like waters and righteousness like an ever-flowing stream. We need to undergird our social and political action with life-transforming and policy-shaping visions of God, humankind, and our planet. Inspired by process theology's vision of an empathetic God, who sides with the marginalized, we can humbly claim our vocation as God's companions in healing the world.

Theology matters in changing hearts, minds, and policies. Theology can be profoundly practical in shaping public policy in a pluralistic society. Witness the theological foundations of the anti-slavery movement in England the United States, the Social Gospel's focus on economic justice, the Civil Rights movement emerging from African-American churches, the anti-apartheid and truth and reconciliation process in South Africa, and the growing climate movement in Christian congregations. Each of these movements emerged from a vision of a lively God who takes sides in the course history, affirms the holiness of creation, feels the pain of the oppressed, challenges the status quo, and needs human agency to embody the divine vision of Shalom. Each of these movements encouraged spiritual humility, recognizing the limitations and imperfections of every theological and political movement and aspiring toward the horizons of a "more perfect union." Each of these movements believed in the possibility of conversion and sought broad coalitions and at times compromises as necessary to approximate God's vision of Shalom in the maelstrom of contrasting political and historical voices.

As the conflation of conservative religion and politics demonstrates, the church can give theological credence to power, domination, and destruction. The church can also baptize bigotry, hatred, and monolithic decision-making as God's way in the world. Believers can look backward to the golden age of theocracies and Christian exceptionalism and forward toward crusade and apocalypse. The church can also provide alternative, earth supportive visions, that put persons ahead of profits and join rights with responsibilities. Grounded in a profoundly relational and open-spirited theology, life-affirming spirituality can inspire, energize, empower, and include.

Following the counsel of Martin Luther King, the church's calling is to be a headlight and not a taillight in responding to the crises of our time. World-affirming and pluralistic theologies awaken us to the moral and spiritual arcs of history flowing in and through us to heal the world. Our beliefs about God can inspire prayer, picketing, protest, and voting. This is public theology at its most profound, humbly seeking to redeem and transform our public places and political decision-making to approximate God's Beloved Community in a pluralistic society where each voice matters and every life is cherished.

THE POLITICAL PROMISE OF PROCESS THEOLOGY

Process theology can energize progressive Christianity and politics. Process theology presents a creative, inspiring, and empowering vision of God in which our vocation is to be God's companions in healing the world. Recognizing that authoritarian images of God promote incivility and scorched earth politics, including the destruction of democratic institutions to achieve religiously-based

6

political goals, process theology presents the contrasting image of God as our intimate companion, promoting freedom, creativity, and diversity, and calling us to partnership in healing the world. A relational God challenges us to overcome divisiveness in a quest for wider circles of partnership, even including those with contrasting viewpoints, to promote the political and social healing we seek.

As a progressive Christian, I seek to follow the way of Jesus, and humbly assert Jesus' way embraces diversity, pluralism, and contrast. The Galilean vision challenges oppression, intolerance, and absolutism while seeing God's love for those who promote these perspectives. Strong in its beliefs, process theology, like the way of Jesus, recognizes the universality of God's revelation and affirms both the legitimacy and limits of protest. Humble, we affirm the humanity of those who oppose our vision and recognize our own temptation to exclude and diminish. Inspired by a life-changing theological vision and heart-awakening spiritual practices, we press on toward the goal of personal, political, and planetary wholeness, realizing that God needs us to prophets in our time.

Process theology affirms a vision of reality that joins individual and social, personal and planetary, diversity and solidarity, contemplation and action, and privacy and politics, grounded in the following affirmations:

1) *Life is profoundly interdependent.* With South African theologians and political activists, process theology affirms the vision of *ubuntu,* "I am because of you." As Martin Luther King affirmed, "We are caught in an inescapable network of mutuality, tied into a single garment of destiny. Whatever affects one directly, affects all indirectly. We are made to live together because of the interrelated structure of reality."[2] In contrast to rugged individualism and nation-first ideologies, process theology asserts that no nation, species, or individual can go it alone. We need one another to flourish as nations and persons. As King asserts, "For some strange reason I cannot be what I ought to be until you are what you ought

---

2   Martin Luther King, *Testament of Hope* (New York: HarperOne), 254.

to be. And you can never be what you ought to be until I am what I ought to me. That's the way God's universe is made."[3]

The interdependence of life reminds us that we all matter. The world is saved one action at a time. Accordingly, we need to get off our couches to act both locally and globally, caring for our neighbor and involving ourselves in public policy for the common good.

2) *Experience and Value Characterize Reality.* When African American mystic and activist Howard Thurman was a youth, growing up in Jim Crow era Daytona Beach, Florida, he was hired to rake leaves by a local merchant. As young Howard raked piles of leaves, the merchant's daughter did what most young children do: she jumped on the piles and scattered them across the lawn. After asking her several times to quit, Howard warned her that he would tell her father if she continued. Angry, she pulled out a hat pin and poked Howard with it. When he let out a cry of pain, she responded with astonishment, "Howard, you can't feel!" As a result of the attitudes of her parents and the white community, she had come to believe that African Americans could not feel pain. "You can't feel!" is the mantra of racism, sexism, homophobia, jingoism, and speciesism. In contrast, process theology asserts that we are part of the living universe. Every creature is a center of emotional experience, encountering the world from its own perspective. Accordingly, process theology asserts that wherever there is experience, there is value that requires our ethical consideration. Whether we speak of chimpanzees, right whales, prenates (fetuses) and their mothers, toddlers separated from their parents on the USA borderlands, enemy combatants, persons dying from the Coronavirus, and those who differ politically from us, the ability to experience pain compels us to think and act ethically even when we must make difficult personal or business decisions. The suffering our

3 Martin Luther King *A Knock at Midnight* (New York: Warner Books, 2000), 208.

actions cause, directly or indirectly, must be part of every political and economic calculus, whether these relate to national security, the judicial system, or economic decisions. In the context of protest and pandemic, African Americans feel and Black Lives Matter!

3) *Creative Transformation is at the Heart of Reality.* Each moment of our lives involves the interplay of past, present, and future. Each moment presents us the opportunity to choose beauty or ugliness, good or evil, and life and death. Each moment involves a call and response in which God presents us with an array of possibilities for the immediate context and the long-term future. Our response adds or subtracts from God's quest for Shalom. The arc of the universe aims at justice and beauty as God seeks to evolve in partnership with humankind's structures of Shalom and healing. God's fidelity is reflected in new mercies that emerge with each new day. (Lamentations 3:22-23) In the dance of creative transformation, the future is open for God and the world. There is no apocalyptic endpoint or predestined outcome to the human adventure. In concert with God, the world moves forward or slips backward, calling forth further divine creativity, compassion, and challenge.

4) *The Interplay of Diversity and Unity Characterize the Universe and Community Life.* Process theology affirms that in each moment of experience the many become one and are increased by one. Diversity and unity merge to create communities and personal histories. Diversity is inherent in the nature of the universe. God parents forth a multi-colored, multi-faceted, and multi-dimensional universe. The founding parents of the United States placed E Pluribus Unum on our national seal to reflect the importance of pluralism, contrast, and diversity in opinion, statecraft, and religion in the nation's identity. Recognizing the limitations of every ethical and public policy perspective, difference is a call to conversation and cooperation. Listening to each other despite the

differences in voice, color, and perspective leads to new solutions and adventurous possibilities. Polarization and incivility go against God's vision of Shalom, whether in politics, relationships, social media, or the workplace. Political practices need to be inspired by a return to the affirmation of the "loyal opposition," the recognition that persons of good will with whom we disagree are often just as patriotic, compassionate, and committed to national wellbeing as us.

5) *God is Personal, Relational, and Inspirational.* God is the ultimate pattern for the universe, our communities, and personal lives. God's nature parents forth change, creativity, freedom, and diversity. God is the "most moved mover," whose love gives birth to the universe in its intricate interdependence and embraces the universe in its creativity and tragic beauty. God is the fellow sufferer who understands and the intimate companion who celebrates. God is the ultimate source of orderly relatedness and creative novelty. Alignment with God moves us from apathy to empathy as we seek to add to the love and beauty of the world. To follow the relational God means to open our hearts to the joy and sorrow of creation and lovingly respond in our quest to heal the institutional structures of our community and nation.

6) *God Loves the World and Wants Us to Love it Too.* God is embodied in all things great and small. God truly does love the world, feeling its joy and responding to its pain. In an open-ended universe, God constantly invites us to move toward horizons of peace, beauty, goodness, and justice. God has "skin in the game." What happens in the world brings joy or sorrow to our Creator and Companion, whose goal is global healing. Healing may require unprecedented changes in behavior as we discovered during the COVID-19 pandemic. As in our personal lives, political and economic surgery may be necessary in terms of significant changes in lifestyle and consumption. But the Spiritual Surgeon always aims at the healing of

persons and institutions rather than scorched earth destruction.

7) *God Needs Our Companionship in Healing the World.* Our open-ended, relational, and creative universe is energized and guided by an open-spirited, intimate, and innovative God. What we do matters to God and to the future. The multiplicity and enormity of challenges we face at the national and planetary level can easily overwhelm us. We can give up hope for the future, focusing only on the wellbeing of our immediate family and community. Yet, God calls us beyond self, family, and nation to world loyalty and planetary transformation. In moments of hopelessness, God invites us to step forward in faith uncertain of the outcome but knowing that without our efforts, the forces of darkness will prevail. Process politics sees the concrete limitations we face as the womb of possibility and horizon of hope. More than that with Teresa of Avila, process theology sees humans as God's hands and feet, furthering God's realm on earth, especially when we find common ground with other seekers after justice and healing.

Inspired by God's intimate companionship and inspiration, we conclude this chapter with this prayer of Harry Emerson Fosdick:

Save us from weak resignation
to the evils we deplore;
let the search for thy salvation
be our glory evermore.
Grant us wisdom, grant us courage,
serving thee whom we adore.

CHAPTER TWO

A MORE PERFECT UNION

I believe that the philosophical insights of the United States Declaration of Independence and Constitution can be illuminated by the process-relational metaphysics of Alfred North Whitehead and his theological followers. The Declaration of Independence and Constitution reflect the creative transformation of the philosophical and religious vision of Enlightenment Deism with that of more traditional Christians. From the beginning, pluralism and change were embedded in the American experiment and the adventures of ideas that gave birth to the quest for a more perfect union.

Whitehead once noted that the pure conservative goes against the nature of the universe. The universe is dynamic and evolving. The evolutionary arc of the universe aims at beauty in the micro and macrocosms. Divine wisdom evolves galaxies, planets, and our earth and non- human and human adventures, reflected in the greater complexity of organisms and human experience and the evolution of religion and morality. The same dynamic was at work in forming the Declaration of Independence and Constitution. Not imprisoned by the past, the Founding Parents sought to embody what they believed to be a new form of government, evolving beyond monarchy, toward a more perfect union of persons, communities, and states. Limited in their own moral perspectives, the authors of the Constitution nevertheless had the foresight to imagine that their successors would have greater insights related to human rights and balancing individualism and community. They recognized that the documents they drafted were incomplete and subject to amendment and interpretation in quest of the more perfect union.

The USA Declaration of Independence begins with an audacious affirmation, one that the USA is still attempting to realize in daily life and political decision-making.

> **We** hold these Truths to be self-evident, that all Men are created equal, that they are endowed by their Creator with certain unalienable Rights, that among these are Life, Liberty,

12

and the Pursuit of Happiness—That to secure these Rights, Governments are instituted among Men.

Each person is valuable, beloved, and gifted by God, without exception. Within each life and every act is the quest for life, liberty, and happiness. There is an Eros toward wholeness, a polestar toward creativity moving through every life. The divinity within is dynamic, passionate, and forward-moving in the historical process.

The moral limitations of the Founding Parents are obvious. Though the Framers imagined a nation of free people, their moral imagination was still stunted and in need of prophetic challenge. From the beginning, our nation fell short of its Founders' dream and needed the freshness and restlessness of divine inspiration aiming at larger and larger circles of equality. Today these circles of divine equality must include non-citizens as well as refugees. They must also include repentance for four hundred years of systemic racism and the ongoing decimation of First Americans.

In words that the Framers did not fully fathom and that we have not fully embodied in American law and social relations, the Preamble of the Constitution sets forth the agenda of a dynamic and evolving body politic, constantly going beyond past moral and political achievements, embodying in imperfect human relationships the moral arc of history.

We the People of the United States, in Order to form a more perfect Union, establish Justice, insure domestic Tranquility, provide for the common defence, promote the general Welfare, and secure the Blessings of Liberty to ourselves and our Posterity, do ordain and establish this Constitution for the United States of America.

The "more perfect Union" is the horizon of possibility, the prophetic discontent with the status quo, not only evident in the writing of the Bill of Rights and future Amendments to the Constitution, but in the ongoing expansion of the circle of human rights to include persons of color, women, immigrants, religious minorities, and the LGBTQ community. Creativity, exploration, and adventure are at the heart of the American vision, even when that vision promotes the inevitable tensions inherent in contrasting visions of reality, religion, lifestyle, and morality. Pluralism and diversity mark the American experiment, despite its glaring failures to embody these values.

Seeking to avoid a return to monarchy, theocracy, and uniformity, anti-Federalists championed a Bill of Rights. These rights protected human freedom in the context of concrete human relationships and our responsibilities as citizens. Rights and responsibilities go hand in hand. The legal history of the United States reflects the quest to maximize freedom and creativity congruent with the common good. Although rights are inalienable, they are always relative. First and Second Amendment rights, for example, are not absolute. While the government guarantees freedom of speech, assembly, press, and religion, the actual practices of religion are limited by the quest for the common good and individual wellbeing. While worship and teaching should be untrammeled, my faith does not entitle me to commit acts of violence or infringement on other peoples' faiths or threaten other peoples' lives as many pastoral leaders did when they insisted on public worship despite the risks of contagion.

This inherent tension between sectarian religious perspectives, the common good, and human rights surfaces today in legal issues related to public prayer and teaching creationist science in the schools, sales of wedding cakes to gay and lesbian couples, conversion therapy, the scope of rights for the LGBTQ community, and coverage for contraception and abortion on health care plans. This same inherent tension is at work in interpretations of Roe v. Wade. Do prenates have rights protected by the Constitution? If so, are these rights absolute and inviolable under all circumstances or do they relate to fetal development, the ability to experience pain, or the health condition of the fetus and/or mother? How do prenatal rights, grounded in process theology's recognition of the universality of value and experience, balance with the "life, liberty, and pursuit of happiness" of women?

While personal prayer has never been outlawed in public schools and students are permitted to form religious and ethical groups on campuses in the USA, do public prayers infringe on those who hold different beliefs, recognizing that generic "one size

14

fits all" prayers seldom satisfy the piety of the religious or those with traditional religious beliefs? As a grandparent and practicing Christian, I object to certain Christian prayers that by implication diminish other peoples' faiths or define certain persons such as members of the LGBTQ community as immoral and in need of conversion just as I would to the poetry of the biblical creation stories being taught as science in biology classes.

THE CENTER IS EVERYWHERE

St. Bonaventure asserted that God is a circle whose center is everywhere and whose circumference is nowhere. The Infinite is intimate. The political is personal. Holiness may be found in the Jerusalem Temple and our houses of worship and sacred spaces, but, as Isaiah discovered, "the whole earth is full of God's glory." (Isaiah 6:3, AP) John's Gospel proclaims that "the true light, which enlightens everyone, was coming into the world" (John 1:9). Revelation, inspiration, and divine favor are inherent in human experience. This democracy of the Spirit is portrayed in Peter's speech on Pentecost:

> In the last days it will be, God declares,that I will pour out my Spirit upon all flesh, and your sons and your daughters shall prophesy, and your young men shall see visions, and your old men shall dream dreams. Even upon my slaves, both men and women, in those days I will pour out my Spirit; and they shall prophesy. (Acts 2:17-18)

Joined with the apostle Paul's affirmation of the university of spiritual gifts and vocation in 1 Corinthians 12, the early Christian movement imagined a spiritual democracy, which like the USA Constitution, was never fully explored or embodied. Congruent with Paul's vision, process theology affirms that God's presence is everywhere. Every moment emerges from the interplay of divine wisdom and creativity, creaturely agency, and the impact of the past. There is, as Quakers assert, a divine light, something of God, in everyone. A minority position among white settlers, William Penn created a "peaceable kingdom" in Pennsylvania when he and the Lenape Turtle Trible of the Delaware Indians signed a peace treaty in 1684. Later, Quaker mystic John Woolman traveled to Indian territories to deepen relationships and learn from America's indigenous peoples. This perception of the divine image of all was enshrined in the USA Constitution and the abolitionist quest championed by British politician William Wilberforce. Inspired by his evangelical experience, Wilberforce came to see that the inherent dignity of enslaved peoples challenged the diabolical nature of slavery. His faith led him and many of his religious contemporaries to lead a moral crusade that eventuated in the passage of the Slave Trade Act of 1807.

For process theologians, the image of God as the center animating all things is both personal and political. Centered and inspired by God, every creature deserves reverence. While issues of power and survival are essential to personal and community survival, the inherent value of human and non-human life requires ethical and political consideration. Moreover, if the circumference of divine love, creativity, and wisdom, is infinite, then no one falls outside the circle of ethical and political concern. Accordingly, process theology advocates a "centered pluralism" in religion, ethics, relationships, politics, and foreign policy. Diversity is essential to reality. In a pluralistic world, no perspective is absolute or final. In fact, the nature of spiritual maturity involves growing in wisdom and spiritual stature in which our own deepest values grow in relationship with the values of others.

Centered pluralism does not suggest that all perspectives equally reflect God's vision. It does assert that the many voices of the body politic are positive, rather than negative, in the evolution of healthy democracies. There are, as the Sufi mystic Rumi exclaimed, a hundred ways to kneel and kiss the ground. Democracies flourish because of diverse opinions. This affirmation of diversity, like the separation of powers of the USA Constitution, places limits on unrestrained profit, power, and uniformity. It checks paternalistic, dominating, and monarchical tendencies, especially among heads of state and majority groups. While there are temporary winners and losers in the pathway of democracy, minority voices must be welcomed as sources of alternative and complementary wisdom, experience, and perspective. Democracy depends on an empathetic listening to the experiences of minorities, underrepresented groups, and politically "inconsequential" communities as much as following the policies established by the privileged and powerful. Painful as it is in community relations and political decision-making, process theology asserts that prophetic visionaries, protesting injustice, are essential to the creation of a more perfect union. Black Lives Matter, March for our Lives, and Global Climate Change protests raise peoples' consciousness and are instrumental in effecting positive political change. They also check the pretensions of those who limit the free exchange of ideas for political gain. Adventures of ideas are constantly at work in history, calling us beyond prejudice to more inclusive and life-affirming visions of democracy.

As I initially wrote these words on Martin Luther King's birthday, the memory of reading a short biography of Martin Luther King with my grandchildren, then ages nine and seven, is fresh. The dreams of Martin Luther King and others of a Beloved Community, embracing and honoring America's great diversity, motivated everyday people of all races to protest, picket, and pray. Like the Hebraic prophets, they visualized an alternative reality to the injustice of Jim Crow and separate but equal statutes. Decades before, USA women marched for the vote motivated by the vision of an equal America. Years after King's freedom marches, persons of faith and religious outsiders sought legal protection and marriage equality for the LGBTQ community following the Stonewall protests. Today, we protest for environmental and racial justice.

One of the great days of my ministerial service occurred when our church voted to be "open and affirming" of the LGBTQ community. We could no longer be silent when religious traditions and legal statutes have traumatized, persecuted, and disenfranchised sexual minorities. With the current marriage of authoritarian religion and politics, we realize that the moral and spiritual arc of history is fragile and must be affirmed as reflective of the diversity of divine creativity and human expression. We recognize that the soul of the USA and other nations is at stake when we turn away from God's vision of Shalom, the diverse Beloved Community God seeks, by the separation of toddlers and infants from their parents at USA borderlands, persecution of undocumented workers and harassing of legal immigrants, and violence against racial minorities by law officers and the implicit promotion of white supremacy by political leaders.

The arc of history bends toward God's vision of Shalom, a nation where all are pilgrims, seeking a more perfect union, bound together in what Martin Luther King, himself influenced by process-relational thought, called the fabric of destiny:

We are caught in an inescapable network of mutuality, tied into a single garment of destiny. Whatever affects one directly, affects all indirectly. We are made to live together because of the interrelated structure of reality.[4]

In the interdependent world envisioned by process theologians and prophetic reformers, we discover the deep truth that our joys and sorrows, successes and failures are one. There is no "other," whose existence is alien to mine.

FROM BINARY BLOVIATION TO CIRCLES OF CIVILITY.

It is impossible to speak of twenty-first century politics without addressing the growing incivility and polarization in national politics not only in North American but also Europe and Australia. When I was growing up during the Eisenhower and Kennedy years, both USA political parties addressed each other as the "loyal opposition." They recognized that they often passionately held contrasting positions about economics, social programs, civil rights legislation, and foreign policy. Yet, despite fundamental differences in political policy, they affirmed each other's patriotism and love of country. Indeed, in the passing of the Civil Rights Act of 1964, social liberal perspectives, championed by President Lyndon Johnson, and small-town conservative perspectives promoted by Republican Leader Everett Dirksen found common cause in the quest for equality. Politicians could disagree, as the saying goes, without being disagreeable! While the USA still had a long way to go in the quest for civil rights, human rights, and social welfare, and LGBTQ rights weren't even an issue in 1964, there was a sense that we can join together, meeting in the middle, to achieve the common good.

4   Martin Luther King, *Testament of Hope*, 254.

In contrast, whether in social media or the Halls of Congress, incivility and demonization of opponents have become the rule of the day. Shouting rather than listening has become normative on the floor of the House and in Facebook communications. Rather than seeking large perspectives, people hunker down in particular political siloes, listening to news aimed at solidifying and supporting their beliefs, nodding approvingly at half-truths, and falsehoods promulgated on social media or from celebrity political commentators and living from one inflammatory tweet to the next.

I recognize that there are a variety of reasons for the collapse of a common, albeit diverse, national vision. At the macro level, mistrust of politicians is global, especially in the wake of Watergate, Iran Contra, and the wars in Vietnam, Iraq, and Afghanistan. Further, the pace of change has been astronomical. In the wake of Vatican II, many Roman Catholics were left spiritually reeling when what they assumed was true and unchanging was jettisoned in favor of new visions of Christianity. Following Roe v. Wade and the Supreme Court affirmation of marriage equality, many conservative Christians felt the tides history threatening to wash away historic norms of their faith.

Fifty years ago, when I was a first-year college student, I read Alvin Toffler's *Future Shock*, which explored the impact of "too much change in too short a time" on persons and societies. In the religious world, Phyllis Tickle asserts that every five hundred years, the church is forced to have a rummage sale to jettison outworn ideas and embrace new ideas to respond to social, political, and technological change. I believe that these days such rummage sales are occurring daily due to the 24/7 news cycle, rapid technological change, real-time global interaction, and the collapse of national isolation exacerbated by the Coronavirus pandemic. Ronald Reagan once touted God's providential creation of a nation separated from the world by two oceans. In the twenty-first century, there is no place to run or hide as Russian operatives determine USA presidential elections, international foes hack into national infrastructure and release fake news to promote polarization, economic decisions made overseas can put thousands of persons out of work, and a virus first identified in a Chinese province can infect and kill tens of thousands of Americans.

In a world of constant technological change and informational bombardment, our powers of adaptation are taxed to the limit and we are tempted to circle the wagons, allowing entrance only to persons like us and ideas that favor our world view. We can empathize with the need to narrow down experience and eliminate cognitive dissonance. Perhaps, Toffler is right in asserting that change has been too rapid. The changing demographic, economic, human rights, and spiritual face of the USA and Northern hemisphere is breathtaking and unnerving. The world is too much with us, and eliminating unwelcome detail can give us a temporary, though false peace, that must be continually nourished by the bullying and bloviation of politicians and marshaling of alternative facts. I know this to be true because at times I am tempted to demonize white nationalists, conservative Christian cheerleaders for Donald Trump, and persons whose intellectual backwardness and political intolerance seem obvious to me.

At such polarizing moments, we need to take seriously the affirmations of process theology in our personal and political lives. Process-relational thinkers recognize the temptations and short-term benefits of both emotional denial and dogmatic combat for the survival of organisms and communities. Yet, these behaviors ultimately destroy community. Truly healthy communities go beyond fear, antagonism, and denial to initiate novelty to match the novelty of the environment. This is both a matter of humility and creativity. Humility is essential for a healthy democracy. In the spirit of theologian Reinhold Niebuhr, we need to recognize our tendencies to absolutize our own positions despite the relativity of every perspective, including our own. Tempted to create spiritual and political idols and demonize our opponents, we are challenged to recognize that we have our treasures in earthen vessels and that God alone is absolute and can command our ultimate allegiance. Faced with the partiality and limitations of even the most enlightened perspectives, we need to recognize the truth in what we perceive to be our neighbor's falsehood and the falsehood embedded in our own most passionate truths. The interplay of God's ubiquitous revelation, the democracy of the spirit, and the limitations of every embodiment of divine inspiration, whether in religion and politics, delivers us from authoritarian religion and the adulation of politicians as God's chosen vehicles for national salvation.

Going from binary polarization and incivility to centered pluralism is the gift of spirituality and stature. Process-relational theologian Bernard Loomer speaks of stature or spiritual size as an essential spiritual and intellectual and, I believe, political virtue in a pluralistic age. According to Loomer,

> By size I mean the stature of a person's soul, the range and depth of his love, his capacity for relationships. I mean the volume of life you can take into your being and still maintain your integrity and individuality, the intensity and variety of outlook you can entertain in the unity of your being without feeling defensive or insecure. I mean the strength of your spirit to encourage others to become freer in the development of their diversity and uniqueness.[5]

Process-relational theology inspires us to become "mahatmas" or large-souled persons, who despite our political differences, can affirm the humanity of those who hold contrasting viewpoints. Recognizing the democracy of inspiration, we welcome and seek to understand diverse viewpoints as potentially contributory to our own evolving understandings of politics and religion. Persons of stature have strong opinions but are also empathetic to persons of equally strong opinions with whom we differ. While we must counter with law and protest challenges to human rights, traumatizing of children, voter suppression, falsehoods that undergird public and foreign policy, and acts of violence perpetrated against religious, sexual, and ethnic minorities, we still must seek to discern the divine light hidden in those who fear and hate. We must diligently discern and nurture the divine light in those who are traumatized and abused and lash out with violence.

Howard Thurman spoke of the wisdom of mystical activism. Motivated by his direct and life-transforming encounter with God, the mystic works for a world in which everyone can experience their

5   Harry James Cargas and Bernard Lee, *Religious Experience and Process Theology.* Mahweh, NJ: PaulistPress. 1976), 70.

21

holiness and the holiness of the world. The mystic challenges social policies that prevent people from experiencing their full humanity, grounded in the divine image while recognizing the divinity of those who perpetrate injustice and oppression. They, too, are God's children.

Process-relational theology affirms the importance of a politics of empathy and compassion. Delivered from the prison of apathy, we can join prayer and protest, grounded in our empathy for the least of these as well as the greatest, seeking a world in which all are pilgrims and none are strangers. We can pray with Jim Manley for a strong spirit of gentleness:

> *Spirit, Spirit of gentleness, blow through the wilderness,*
> *Calling and free.*
> *Spirit, Spirit of restlessness, blow through my placidness,*
> *Wind, wind on the sea...*
> *You call from tomorrow, you break ancient schemes,*
> *from the bondage of sorrow the captives dream dreams,*
> *our women see visions, our men clear their eyes*
> *with bold new decisions your people arise.*[6]

---

6 Jim Manley, "Spirit of Gentleness." (Used by permission.)

CHAPTER THREE

THE ARC OF JUSTICE AND BEAUTY

Within the maelstrom of history resides the upward movement of life. Creation is lively, dynamic, and on the move. There is an inner Eros, providentially moving within our lives and institutions. Its power is relational and works within chance, intentionality, and synchronicity, calling us forward toward horizons of Shalom. Alfred North Whitehead claims that "the teleology of the universe is aimed at beauty," whether we are describing the emergence and evolution of galaxies and planets, the flora and fauna of the earth, or the growth of human civilization.[7] Working patiently to nurture creativity and freedom, God moves through each creature and every moment aiming at beauty and justice.

Eighty years before Whitehead, surveying a nation in conflict over slavery, Unitarian abolitionist Theodore Parker proclaimed:

> Look at the facts of the world. You see a continual and progressive triumph of the right. I do not pretend to understand the moral universe, the arc is long, my eye reaches but little ways. I cannot calculate the curve and complete the figure by the experience of sight; I can divine it by conscience. But from what I see I am sure it bends toward justice.

Both Whitehead and Parker can be accused of being overly optimistic in their understanding of history, given the twenty-first century realities of climate change denial; incivility, polarization, and the growing threat of white nationalism in the United States; inhumane USA border policies and seventy million people worldwide forced from their homeland due to drought, malnutrition, violence, and political instability. Those of us seeking God's realm "on earth as it is in heaven" often feel like the Breton fisherman's prayer that confesses "God, the sea is so great and my boat is so small." Yet, despite our apparent helplessness and hopelessness in the face of malignant political powers greater than ourselves, the

---

7   Alfred North Whitehead, *The Adventures of Ideas* (New York: Free Press, 1961(, 265.

prayer which President John F. Kennedy placed on his desk continues as an image of hope.

> Thy sea, O God, so great,
> My boat so small.
> It cannot be that any happy fate
> Will me befall
> Save as Thy goodness opens paths for me
> Through the consuming vastness of the sea.
> Thy winds, O God, so strong,
> So slight my sail.
> How could I curb and bit them on the long
> And saltry trail,
> Unless Thy love were mightier than the wrath
> Of all the tempests that beset my path?
> Thy world, O God, so fierce,
> And I so frail.
> Yet, though its arrows threaten oft to pierce
> My fragile mail,
> Cities of refuge rise where dangers cease,
> Sweet silences abound, and all is peace.

This prayer reflects the hopeful realism of the Hebraic prophets. Injustice abounds and dreams are deferred. The poor are sold into slavery, farms foreclosed, and dishonesty abounds in high places. Religious institutions have turned from compassion to embrace power and wealth as the highest goods. Priests have become cheerleaders for unjust pollical practices and have identified morally bankrupt political leaders as God's chosen. Yet, the prophets know God will have the final word. Justice will be done. The wealthy, who have silenced the voices of the vulnerable will experience a famine on hearing God's word. Despite our uncertainty, God will make a way where there is no way. The moral and spiritual arc will eventually triumph and invite us to participate in new horizons of justice.

Speaking for God's vision, the prophets imagine an alternative future, the realization of God's dream of Shalom in the challenges of life. A nation will arise where justice will roll down like waters and righteousness like an everflowing stream.

African American spiritual guide Howard Thurman asserted that the mystical encounter with the Living God inspires us to challenge the forces of injustice. Energized and enlivened by the experience of divine intimacy, mystics seek a world in which everyone can experience the fullness of life. Whatever stands in the way must be challenged by today's prophets. Injustice stunts our imaginations, creativity, and experience of beauty. The fullness of life, denied to the vulnerable and oppressed, requires structures of justice in the courthouse, boardroom, political arena, educational system, and borderlands.

Sensitive to the divine pathos, God's experience of suffering, the mystic awakens to the cries of the poor, vulnerable, forgotten, and abused. Their pain is God's pain. Their voices are God's voices. The agony inflicted on them crucifies Jesus. Within the soul-stunting realities of environmental and political injustice, the mystic experiences God's aim at beauty, which may be deferred by human recalcitrance, but which can never ultimately be thwarted. The arc of justice and beauty moving within human history and the non-human world pushes us toward greater and greater circles of compassion and care, reminding us that injustice anywhere is a threat to justice everywhere.

While God's love embraces all creation, God has a special concern for the forgotten, maligned, abused, and disenfranchised. Injustice and diminishment detract from the incarnation of divine Shalom in the world and deface the inherent beauty and value of each creature. Unjust political structures stand in the way of God's aim at beauty in our lives and communities. In describing the impact of human choices on God's vision, Whitehead notes:

> God's purpose is always embodied in particular ideals relevant to the actual state of the world...Every act leaves the world with a deeper or fainter impress God. He then passes to his next relation to the world with enlarged, or diminished, presentation of ideal values.[8]

---

8 Alfred North Whitehead, *Religion in the Making* (New York: Meridian Books, 1972), 152.

What we do in the political arena matters to God. God needs our companionship to realize God's vision of Shalom. As small as our boat may seem, each act aimed at the realization of justice and beauty transforms the world and expands the scope of divine activity.

JUST BEAUTY

Process theology sees politics as spiritual formation. We are formed by our communities and our public policies reflect our values and priorities. Beyond binary divisions of left and right, process theology challenges us to be stewards of beauty. Political involvement is not for the faint-hearted. But, persons of spiritual strength and stature, pursue policies that maximize beauty and minimize suffering, at home and abroad, including non-humans as well as humans.

Today, we must see political involvement as our "great work" as citizens seeking to create structures of beauty and justice. Seeking the right blend of order and novelty, creativity and stability, and freedom and law, to promote the common good, structures of beauty and justice put persons ahead of profits and environment over economic gain, knowing that the cost of eco-injustice outweighs, and should be factored into, economic growth and foreign policy.

Aware of conflicting interests and our tendency toward self-interest, politically awakened citizens and leaders must ask questions such as:

Does this policy add to the beauty of the world?

Does this policy take into consideration the marginalized and voiceless?

Does this policy challenge systemic racism which puts lives in danger and threatens persons' ability to fulfill their destiny as God's beloved children?

Does this action contribute to planetary wellbeing not just in the present moment but for generations ahead?

How can we promote a symphony of perspectives, creative of a great civilization?

How do we balance profit with cost to the marginalized, and to the human and non-human world?

26

How does our nation expand the circle of justice to include other nations and the non-human world?

How do we join the potentially coercive nature of justice-seeking with affirmation of creativity and beauty?

Beauty and justice are concrete, and cannot be understood in terms of abstract moral principles. Abstractions, apart from the consideration of human experience, promote violence and polarization. While we may have strong opinions about the morality of abortion and physician-assisted suicide, structural injustice, religious freedom, gun ownership, and LGBTQ rights, public policy must be grounded in empathy, most especially toward those whom Jesus described as the "least of these" but also including those fearful of social transformation. As stewards of beauty and justice in the political realm, our calling is to transcend frantic self-interest to attain peaceful reflection that comes from self-transcendence and identification of our wellbeing with the healing of creation. In that spirit, we conclude this chapter with words of a Navajo blessing:

With beauty before me may I walk.
With beauty behind me may I walk.
With beauty above me may I walk.
With beauty all around me, may I walk.

CHAPTER FOUR

THE POLITICS OF IMPERFECTION

One of Whitehead's most provocative statements involves his description of the character and quality of God's presence in the world. While Whitehead affirms the unambiguous goodness of God, reflected in God's quest for beauty as well as God's loving and empathetic care for each creature, Whitehead also notes that:

> The initial stage of the [subjective] aim is rooted in the nature of God, and its completion depends on the self-causation of the [actual occasion as] subject-superject. This function of God is analogous to the remorseless working of things in Greek and Buddhist thought. The initial aim is the best for that impasse. But if the best be bad, then the ruthlessness of God can be personified as Ate, the goddess of mischief. The chaff is burnt.[9]

While not directly related to political decision-making, Whitehead makes the claim that the intensity and quality of God's presence in the world are related to the decisions of creatures. The concrete world is the womb of possibility. But, with concreteness also comes limitation, even for God. God's vision of Shalom is embodied in the recalcitrance as well as the nobility of flesh and blood creatures.

Politics is appropriately described as "art of the possible." While it is true that "where there is no vision, the people perish" (Proverbs 29:18, KJV) our visions take shape in the actual world of budgetary limitation, conflicting viewpoints, past national history and current political decisions, and the tragic necessity of justly meted out coercion to maintain the order necessary for communal wellbeing. Sadly, governments must at times use violence to protect national integrity and ensure the safety of their citizens. As people of faith, we are commanded to forgive our enemies, but may still need to incarcerate criminals for the public good. Followers of Jesus are mandated to welcome strangers, but hospitality and

---

9   Alfred North Whitehead, *Process and Reality: Corrected Edition* (New York: Free Press, 1978), 244.

compassion must be mated with preserving the integrity of national borders, providing orderly immigration processes, and preventing malign forces from crossing the border. These, and many other, political decisions, necessitate compromise and less than ideal implementations of law to embody the "best for that impasse." Still, our priority is to seek justice, minimize the use of force, and seek non-violent and preventative solutions to social ills.

Process theology affirms God's quest for beauty in the lives of persons and institutions. We seek not only a "great society," but a society that promotes beauty and largeness of spirit. We must always aim for a more perfect union, recognizing that all our achievements fall short of God's vision of Shalom. In seeking to be companions of God in healing the world and to imitate God's quest for beauty in our personal and corporate behavior, we need to recognize that the achievement of these goals is always partial and often requires choosing imperfect solutions that pave the way for the perfect union we seek.

The moral and spiritual arcs of history flow through us, requiring us to seek the highest good in our personal and political lives. We cannot be content with mediocrity and injustice. The suffering of any child through injustice is an affront to God and our moral and spiritual inclinations. The words of Micah and Amos challenge and condemn as well as inspire and energize individuals and political systems alike.

> God has told you, O mortal, what is good, and what does God require of you, but to do justice and to love kindness, and walk humbly with your God. (Micah 6:8)
> Take away from me the noise of your songs; I will not listen to the melody of your harps. But let justice roll down like waters, and righteousness like an ever-flowing stream. (Amos 5:23-24)

Without prophetic ideals, we are doomed to injustice and exploitation. Conversely, failure to consider concrete political and economic limitations, embodied in the conflicts and compromises of legislative decision-making, renders our ideals irrelevant. The deepest of human relationships, those of parenting and marriage, require idealism and the highest moral standards but are imperfectly embodied by imperfect persons seeking to love other imperfect persons in imperfect environments.

Recent historians have critiqued Abraham Lincoln's reticence to enact the Emancipation Proclamation until the Union scored a major military victory. They have judged Lincoln for initially limiting emancipation to the Confederate states and not enacting the Proclamation on the border states. Lincoln wanted to abolish slavery. But, in his mind, the only way to abolish slavery was to preserve the Union. Lincoln believed that the continued reality of two nations on American soil would have likely ensured the existence of slavery for decades to come. In the USA, we are still struggling to achieve the unity and equality Lincoln sought over 150 years ago.

In similar fashion, war should only be entered into at the last resort and with clear ethical and military justification. Recent history has shown that the USA's wars in Vietnam, Iraq, and Afghanistan have been unwarranted and have cost thousands of lives, permanently injured and traumatized our soldiers, and exhausted resources that could have been better used on infrastructure, health care, education, and quality of life. Still, there are moments when war is the best for an historical impasse. Had the United States not entered World War II, Hitler might have occupied the totality of Europe and continued his genocide of the Jewish people.

The biblical tradition suggests that even God must find common ground with imperfect humankind. In the legend of Sodom and Gomorrah, God initially states that the cities will be preserved if fifty righteous people can be found. Perhaps more realistic than God, Abraham bargains for twenty and then ten, and God agrees. Sadly, although not even ten can be found, as described in this mythical story unrelated to issues of homosexuality, God is willing to adapt God's vision to the realities of human imperfection.

Humility as well as pragmatism demand that we seek the more perfect union through finding common ground with those whose positions differ from our own. Many political idealists rightly complain that the Affordable Care Act (ACA) did not go far enough in its quest for health insurance for all United States citizens. The current debates between "Medicare for all" and "Medicare for all who want it," preserving the option of private employer-based insurance, reflect the challenge to seek the best for a particular impasse and the ambiguity of every quest for perfection in political decision-making. The passage of the ACA was a major factor in Democrats losing the House and the Senate. The passage of "Medicare for all" will no doubt altar some persons' health insurance and will create unemployment for thousands in the private insurance industry. But, if healthcare is a human right, certain sacrifices will be morally justified.

In speaking of the inevitability of conflict, Whitehead notes that life is robbery, and someone must pay the price for another's benefit. Whitehead is adamant that ethically speaking sacrifices must be justified, and the moral and personal benefits must outweigh others' sacrifices.

We must aspire for the achievement of beauty of experience and that often requires doing the right thing regardless of consequences. We must remember the moral angst of Corrie ten Boom, author of *The Hiding Place*. A conservative Christian, committed to following the Ten Commandments, including "thou shalt not bear false witness," ten Boom nevertheless chose to lie to Nazi soldiers to protect the Jews hidden in her family's residence. Among politicians who treasure honesty and integrity, there is always the tension between discovering the absolutely "right" solution, achieving the greatest good for the greatest number, and preserving national wellbeing, knowing even our most irenic choices will create some degree of suffering.

Compromise reflects the best for certain impasses, provided we do not forsake our ideals or abandon the quest for justice, especially for those who have been marginalized and marked by our nation's sins of slavery, sexism, genocide of indigenous peoples, and persecution of the LGBTQ community. There are times when we must go beyond pragmatism and work toward a political realm "on earth as it is in heaven." This urgency of hope is at work in responding to global climate change. Given the ongoing climate denial championed by many conservative Christians and the current rolling back of environmental protection policies, the next United States leader, as well as leaders of other nations, may have to act unilaterally to ensure planetary survival if legislative support is lacking.

Finding common ground is essential for the flourishing of democracy. But, common ground requires fidelity to the truth, commitment to factuality, recognition of our imperfection, and willingness to honor the "loyal opposition," grounded in recognition of our common identity as God's beloved children and our willingness to look beyond our ideologies to achieve the greater good for the community as a whole. In short supply in the current USA political environment, finding common ground requires learning from contrasting positions that complement and refine our own position. Accepting good-hearted critiques of our own positions prevents us from making unnecessary mistakes as we expand our vision of political possibility. Communication and flexibility are essential, and in imitation of God's relationship to the world, we must balance our creativity and initiative with receptivity to others' viewpoints.

The final words of Alfred North Whitehead's *Adventures of Ideas* portray history in terms of the slow but steady impact of ideals on human civilization.

> At the heart of the nature of things, there are always the dream of youth and the harvest of tragedy. The Adventure of the Universe as One starts with the dream and reaps tragic beauty. This is the secret of the union of Zest with Peace: - That the suffering attains its end in a Harmony of Harmonies. The immediate experience of this Fact, with its union of Youth and Tragedy, is the sense of Peace. In this way the World receives its persuasion towards such perfections as are possible for its diverse individual occasions.[10]

Every compassionate and humble parent, partner, and political leader knows that pain is embedded in personal relationships. A degree of suffering and sacrifice attends every important political decision. Some values must be sacrificed to achieve the greatest good possible. Suffering is inevitable in the quest for the right balance of order and novelty, stability and change, hospitality, and national integrity. But politician and citizen alike must be willing to bear the burden of pain when it is unavoidable in terms of the

10 Alfred North Whitehead, *Adventures of Ideas* (New York: Free Press, 1961), 294.

consequences of our best intentions embodied in political decision-making. We must choose to feel the pain we unintentionally
cause without being debilitated and thus incapable of making the
best decisions for our time and place. Without empathy for the pain
we indirectly cause others, justice in the body politic is impossible.
Perhaps God even feels this pain when God experiences the pain
of complex creatures such as ourselves – the pain we experience
and the pain we cause – as a result of God's evolutionary aim to
create a world capable of supporting experiences of beauty, wonder,
creativity, and sacrifice.

Recognizing our quest for justice and beauty in an imperfect
world, let us affirm the spirit of John Greenleaf Whittier's prayer
in this updated paraphrase:

> *Dear God and Parent of us all*
> *forgive our foolish ways;*
> *reclothe us in our rightful mind,*
> *in purer lives, our service find,*
> *in deeper reverence, praise.*

CHAPTER FIVE

FROM SELF-INTEREST TO WORLD LOYALTY

Alfred North Whitehead noted that a person's character is formed according to their deepest convictions. What we believe can shape how we act. Our personal and corporate beliefs shape our political involvement and national policies. The environmental movement championed by President Barack Obama was grounded in the recognition of climate science and the value of human and non-human species, whose continued wellbeing requires changed behaviors and personal and national sacrifice. The passage of the Affordable Care Act was motivated by the belief that health care is a human right, not an option to be determined by the ability to pay. In recent years, immigration and environmental policies heralded by the Trump Administration have been grounded in America First and economic ideologies that see security and homogeneity as well as economic interests as more compelling than compassion and earth care. Focus on national interests over international partnerships, an emphasis on individualism rather than interdependence inspired Brexit and USA withdrawal from the Paris Accords.

Process theology focuses on the intricate interplay of individuality and interdependence. The whole creation conspires to create each moment of experience. No moment or person is self-made. Conversely, our actions radiate across the universe, shaping the lives of our nearest companions and indirectly both nation and planet. The intricate and dynamic interdependence of life leads Whitehead to make the following affirmations:

1) World consciousness emerges with the emergence of religious maturity. Mature faith evolves from fear and obedience to imitation and creativity. "The new, and almost profane, concept of the goodness of God replaces the older emphasis on the will of God...You study [God's] goodness in order to be like [God].[11]

---

11 Alfred North Whitehead, *Religion in the Making*, 40.

2) In going from individuality to social awareness, a person finds fullness of life in "merging its claim with that of the objective universe. Religion is world loyalty."[12]

3) The quest for peace takes us beyond self-centeredness to identification with wider circles of care. "Peace is self-control at its widest, - at the 'width' where the self has been lost and interest has been transferred to co-ordinations wider than personality."[13]

Healthy relatedness takes us beyond our self-interest to care for others. I regularly tutor at my grandchildren's elementary school. I could be doing other things, but involvement in the education of other people's children is more important to me than extra free time. Sadly, each time I enter the school, I rehearse what I might do if there were an active shooter threat. While I might be inclined to run for my life, I imagine finding a way to confront and neutralize the shooter, even if it means sacrificing my life to protect my grandchildren and their classmates. As I was completing this text, I spent the majority of my day homeschooling them during the Coronavirus pandemic, affirming that their wellbeing is as important as my own professional and pastoral projects. I choose to wear a mask in public not out of convenience but to promote the wellbeing of others and eliminate the spread of the Coronavirus.

Jesus proclaimed that those who put safety and security above all else will lose their spiritual lives, while those who lose their lives for the sake of Jesus' mission will save them! In the biblical tradition, the person most pitied is the self-made man, whose idolatry of independence cuts him off from the wellsprings of divine grace and caring relationships.

Spiritual and ethical maturity involves the ongoing and widening of care for others and the willingness to sacrifice time, talent, and treasure for the greater good. The greater good involves care in the immediate moment for persons in need. It also involves sacrificing present gratification for the wellbeing of future generations.

12 Ibid., 59.
13 Alfred North Whitehead, *Adventures in Ideas*, 285.

Today, the times demand moving from self-interest to world loyalty on the individual and national stage. Our individual well-being is important but wholeness of life occurs only when we see others' good as important as our own, beginning with our immediate family and extending to our immediate communities, nation, and beyond. National self-interest must give way to global concern. What happens in China in January 2020, whether economically, militarily, or in terms of the Coronavirus shapes the quality of life on Cape Cod. What the USA does in terms of environmental policy shapes the survival of non-human species, shoreline cities across the globe, drought conditions in Africa, and forest fire seasons Australia.

As Reinhold Niebuhr notes, individual self-interest is often sacrificed for and replaced by national aggrandizement. Yet, though national sovereignty is important, it is always penultimate. As Matthew 25 asserts, the Messiah will judge the nations on how they treat the hunger, naked, imprisoned, and thirsty. Nations are morally accountable, too, and the times call for public policies that take us from nation-first ideologies to planet-first practices.

Politics as a communal quest for the common good must widen our understanding of the commons. The era of lifeboat ethics has passed. There is no place to hide in terms of climate catastrophe or nuclear war. All political decisions are now global as well as regional and global wellbeing must be taken into consideration in terms of tax, environmental, trade, and military policies.

Given the growing impact of nation-first ideologies and polarization in the body politic of most nations, the dream of an interdependent world in which nations care for the planet with the same commitment as national sovereignty seems unrealistic. Yet, the task of lived theology involves moving from faith to action. Environmental activist Bill McKibben, founder of 350.org asserts that responding to the environmental crisis may be the vocation of the church in our time. Recognizing the intricate relationship between environmental and justice issues, I assert that ecojustice is the church's great work. The poor of the earth, both in the USA and other developed countries suffer most from climate change and pandemic. They are most at risk in terms of polluted air, toxic waterways, and rising oceans.

Public policy needs to become planet policy as we consider the impact on persons across the globe, the vulnerable of our own nation, and generations of unborn children. With an enlarged personal and political vision, we will experience the peace that comes from expanding heart and soul to embrace the wondrous and beautiful adventures of this good earth as we pray with the Psalmist:

Let everything that breathes praise God! (Psalm 150:6)

CHAPTER SIX

THE CHOICE IS LIFE

As they pilgrim from a scattered people toward becoming a nation, the God of Adventure poses two options for the Hebraic people.

> See, I set before you life and prosperity, death and destruction... Now choose life so that you and your children may live, that you may love the Lord your God, listen to his voice, and hold fast to him. (Deuteronomy 30:15, 20)

Although we do not aspire to be a theocracy, these words still ring true. For those whose lives are guided by spiritual values, there is wisdom in the process theology's affirmation that God is present, providentially guiding all things, and at work in the lives of those who claim to be seekers, agnostics, and atheists, as well as those who identify themselves as persons of faith. The arc of justice and beauty is toward life in its fullness. The movement from self-interest to world loyalty aims at abundant life for all creation, not just humanity. Each moment of personal and political decision-making moves us closer to life or death for ourselves and our planetary companions. Recognizing that the future of the planet is now in our hands, the Bulletin of the Atomic Scientists has updated its Doomsday Clock every January since 1947. In 1947, the first setting was seven minutes till midnight. In January 2020, the clock was updated from 11:58 p.m. to 11:58.20, due to a growing threat of nuclear war due to the realities of climate change and nation-first policies. Due to national and geopolitical politics, we are, poetically and possibly literally speaking, just 100 seconds from doomsday.

God calls each person and institution to choose life. The choice of life isn't always clear and often we must choose the best for the impasse, knowing that certain values must be sacrificed for what we presume to be higher values for ourselves and the common good. God's aim directs us toward wholeness, beauty, and justice. We can never fully or clearly discern the best options in a dynamic and interdependent world populated by people of good and ill will, imperfect and at times differing in perspective, all of whom are touched by God.

The circles of life radiate through our personal lifespan to our families, communities, and the planet. What seems good now may not be good in the long haul for ourselves, families, or planets. We must humbly look toward the broadest horizons of planetary and community wellbeing. Still, we must choose, hoping to be on the side of the angels.

Often our personal and public policy choices between life and death involve two significant options, both of whom involve important values. For example, when I choose to take an afternoon to write, I opt out of going to a movie with my wife or playing soccer or reading with my grandchildren. When our church suspends worship in a time of pandemic, we choose the wellbeing of persons with risk factors and the wellbeing of the community over the joy of public worship. When a woman, consulting with her family and medical caregivers, chooses to have an abortion, she is ending the life of an experiencing being, with possibilities before them. The termination of a pregnancy is often more complicated than those in the anti-abortion movement admit. The prenate's health may be in doubt or the woman's future is at a crossroads. Process theology recognizes that both the woman and the prenate are centers of value and experience. Yet choices need to be made. Public policy must join principle with the concreteness of human experience and our impact on the environment. Reproductive health and the rights of women to bodily integrity and social equality must be preserved. We must also recognize that prenates are living beings and that their current complexity of experience requires moral consideration. At the very least, the termination of a pregnancy should be done painlessly and after ethical consideration by the woman in concert with physicians, counselors, loved ones, and spiritual guides.

Conservative Christians claiming to be the victims of discrimination has become a political issue in the United States. Some of their concerns bound on false martyrdom. Marriage equality and rights to the LGBTQ community do not compromise any person's faith or marital fidelity. Heterosexuals, after all, have done enough to jeopardize heterosexual marriage as the example of certain national leaders makes clear. In no way should the rights of the LGBTQ community be abridged by conservative Christian politicians. Our concept of morality and religious freedom do not give us the right to persecute those who differ from us.

Other conservative Christians champion teaching literal understandings of creation in public schools. Teaching evolution in a science class is not an attack on the Christian faith. Evolution, like climate change, is a fact, despite differing theistic and non-theistic interpretations of the process. Teaching various creation stories in a pluralistic society is appropriate, but solely in liberal arts classes where students can read Genesis alongside Hindu and First American cosmologies.

The issue of funding of contraception as a part of health care plans is perhaps more complicated. A pluralistic society must always recognize conscientious objection in relationship with what persons perceive to be unjust wars and laws. Those who object to a policy often pay the price and should be willing to do so. As a conscientious objector for religious purposes during the Vietnam war, I spent the time I would have served in the military working with vulnerable youth. Those conservative Christians who object to paying for others' contraception and abortions should be required to contribute an equal sum to medical services for infants and young children as their alternate payment, while women's reproductive health services can be funded publicly. In this way, we preserve the common good and current laws and provide for conscientious objection.

While there are many life and death issues before us as citizens, the most crucial one facing humankind today is global climate change. This takes us from personal and national self-interest to world loyalty. As environmentalist Bill McKibben avers, the best thing an individual can do to respond to climate change is to quit being an individual. This applies to national sovereignty as well as individual behaviors. The USA's individualistic nation-first withdrawal from the Paris Accords borders on the demonic. It is a clear choice for planetary death to achieve short-term profit and ideological gain. Weakening of environmental protections in the USA is equally diabolical in its choice of death to rivers, wetlands, ponds, species, and ultimately humankind and the ecosphere. There is little ambiguity in climate science research. Legitimate climate scientists agree that human-caused climate change is a reality, though they may disagree regarding its pace.

Adapting public policy to the realities of climate science has obviously benefited our environment. When I first lived in Southern California, the atmosphere was dense with smog. The impact of auto emission legislation in California and across the USA has radically improved air quality. In responding to climate change, national sovereignty and personal freedom must be limited to ensure planetary survival for generations to come. Certain freedoms and lifestyle practices must be sacrificed for the greater good either voluntarily or through national and international law. We must in the USA begin to lower our carbon footprint, to live like Europeans in terms of fossil fuel use, while at the same time ensuring that the majority world has suitable housing, technology, education, and transportation. The developed nations must sacrifice significantly for planetary wellbeing and the wellbeing of those in the impoverished majority world.

Choosing life means for us to live more simply so that others, including non-human species, may live. God loves the 400 Right Whales near extinction and the Sudanese refugee living at a subsistent level as much as God loves overweight North Americans. Choosing life means spiritual and economic decluttering so that others may enjoy abundant life in the future. Changes in public policy and our attitudes toward national sovereignty must occur if our planet is to support life.

In the dynamic, interdependent, pluralistic, and divinely inspired world envisioned by process theology, our calling is toward beauty, justice, and abundant life. Many paths lie ahead as we seek to be God's partners in global and national healing. In politics, choices must be made, but these choices, grounded in the interplay of policy, ethics, and concrete realities must be guided by the universal quest, as Whitehead notes, to live, then to live well, and finally to live better. This is a spiritual as well as economic and legal quest as we commit to God's holy adventure of personal, national, and planetary wholeness. Let us go forth guided by John Henry Newman's prayer:

Lead kindly light amid the encircling gloom.
The far shore I do not ask to see,
Just one step enough for me.

TOPICAL LINE DRIVES
Straight to the Point in under 44 Pages

All Topical Line Drives volumes are priced at $5.99 print and $2.99 in all ebook formats.

Available

The Authorship of Hebrews: The Case for Paul	David Alan Black
What Protestants Need to Know about Roman Catholics	Robert LaRochelle
What Roman Catholics Need to Know about Protestants	Robert LaRochelle
Forgiveness: Finding Freedom from Your Past	Harvey Brown, Jr.
Process Theology: Embracing Adventure with God	Bruce Epperly
Holistic Spirituality: Life Transforming Wisdom from the Letter of James	
	Bruce Epperly
The Eucharist: Encounters with Jesus at the Table	Robert D. Cornwall
The Authority of Scripture in a Postmodern Age: Some Help from Karl Barth	
	Robert D. Cornwall
Rendering unto Caesar	Chris Surber
The Caregiver's Beattitudes	Robert Martin
I'm Right and You're Wrong	Steve Kindle
Words of Woe: Alternative Lectionary Texts	Robert D. Cornwall
Stewardship: God's Way of Recreating the World	Steve Kindle
Those Footnotes in Your New Testament	Thomas W. Hudgins
Jonah: When God Changes	Bruce G. Epperly
Ruth & Esther: Women of Agency and Adventure	Bruce G. Epperly
God the Creator: The Variety of Christian Views on Origins	Henry Neufeld
Choosing Life	Jay McDaniel & John B. Cobb Jr.
Beauty and Process Theology	Patricia Adams Farmer

(The titles of planned volumes may change before release.)

Generous Quantity Discounts Available
Dealer Inquiries Welcome
Energion Publications — P.O. Box 841
Gonzalez, FL 32560
Website: http://energionpubs.com
Phone: (850) 525-3916